Caribou Migration

by Kari Schuetz

BLASTOFF! READERS
3

BELLWETHER MEDIA • MINNEAPOLIS, MN

Note to Librarians, Teachers, and Parents:

Blastoff! Readers are carefully developed by literacy experts and combine standards-based content with developmentally appropriate text.

Level 1 provides the most support through repetition of high-frequency words, light text, predictable sentence patterns, and strong visual support.

Level 2 offers early readers a bit more challenge through varied simple sentences, increased text load, and less repetition of high-frequency words.

Level 3 advances early-fluent readers toward fluency through increased text and concept load, less reliance on visuals, longer sentences, and more literary language.

Level 4 builds reading stamina by providing more text per page, increased use of punctuation, greater variation in sentence patterns, and increasingly challenging vocabulary.

Level 5 encourages children to move from "learning to read" to "reading to learn" by providing even more text, varied writing styles, and less familiar topics.

Whichever book is right for your reader, Blastoff! Readers are the perfect books to build confidence and encourage a love of reading that will last a lifetime!

This edition first published in 2019 by Bellwether Media, Inc.

No part of this publication may be reproduced in whole or in part without written permission of the publisher. For information regarding permission, write to Bellwether Media, Inc., Attention: Permissions Department, 6012 Blue Circle Drive, Minnetonka, MN 55343.

Library of Congress Cataloging-in-Publication Data

Names: Schuetz, Kari, author.
Title: Caribou Migration / by Kari Schuetz.
Description: Minneapolis, MN : Bellwether Media, Inc., 2019. | Series:
   Blastoff! readers. Animals on the move | Audience: Age 5-8. | Audience:
   Grade K to 3. | Includes bibliographical references and index.
Identifiers: LCCN 2017061810 (print) | LCCN 2018005322 (ebook) | ISBN
   9781626178144 (hardcover : alk. paper) | ISBN 9781681035550 (ebook)
Subjects: LCSH: Caribou--Migration--Juvenile literature.
Classification: LCC QL737.U55 (ebook) | LCC QL737.U55 S354 2019 (print) | DDC 599.65/81568--dc23
LC record available at https://lccn.loc.gov/2017061810

Editor: Paige V. Polinsky   Designer: Jeffrey Kollock

Printed in the United States of America, North Mankato, MN

Table of Contents

Caribou

Caribou are **Arctic** animals on the move. These large deer travel between summer and winter homes.

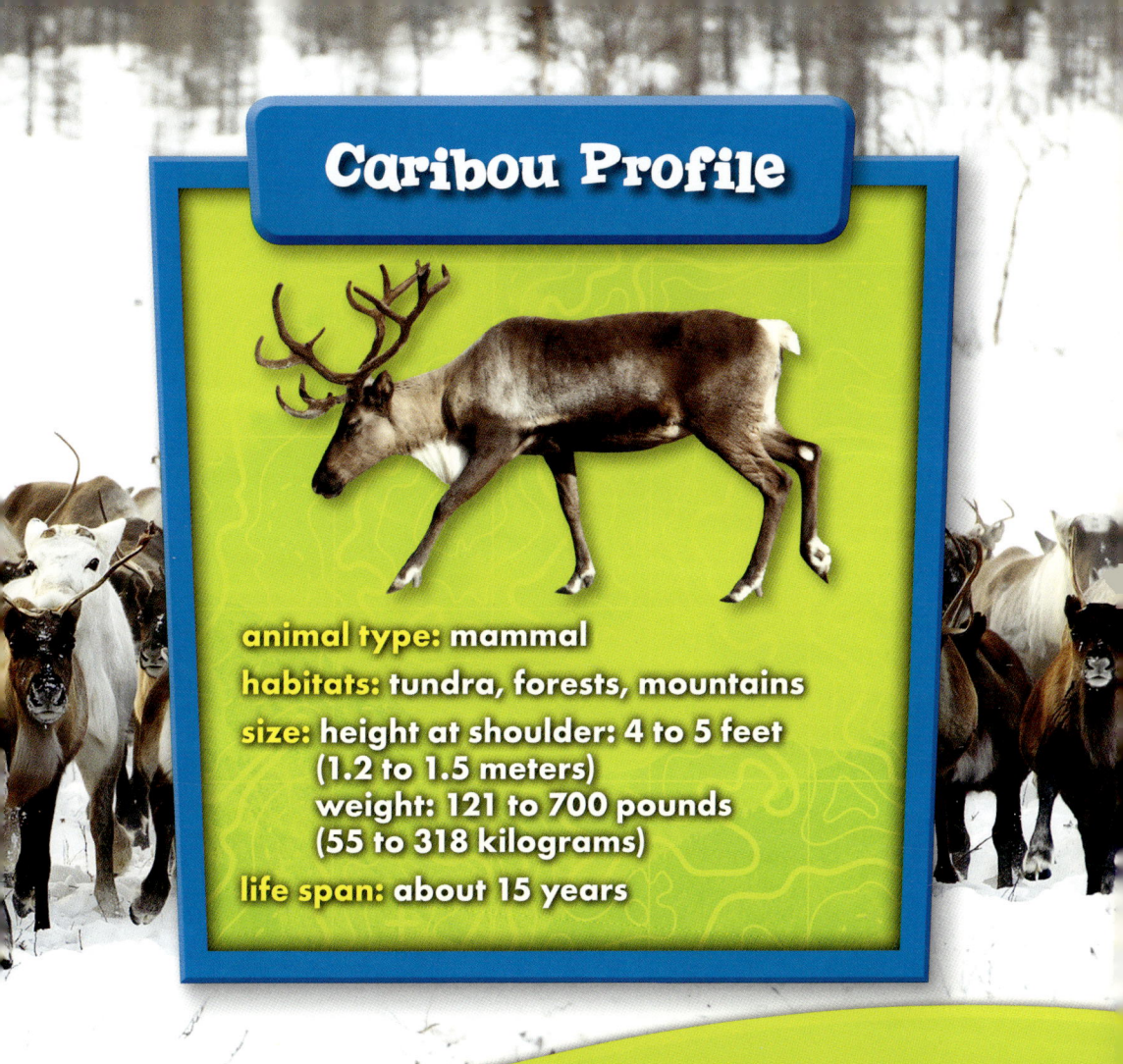

Caribou Profile

animal type: mammal

habitats: tundra, forests, mountains

size: height at shoulder: 4 to 5 feet (1.2 to 1.5 meters)
weight: 121 to 700 pounds (55 to 318 kilograms)

life span: about 15 years

Alaska's Porcupine **herd** can cross 3,000 miles (4,828 kilometers) in one year. No other land **mammals** cover as much ground!

Caribou dress for the season. They wear thick coats in winter. Their **hooves** harden to dig in snow.

In summer, caribou lose some of their hair. Their hooves grow **spongy** pads to cross soft ground.

Many caribou spend spring in the **tundra**. In late June, swarms of mosquitoes and other biting flies attack.

Adult caribou and their **calves** must escape. They move to cool mountains and windy coasts.

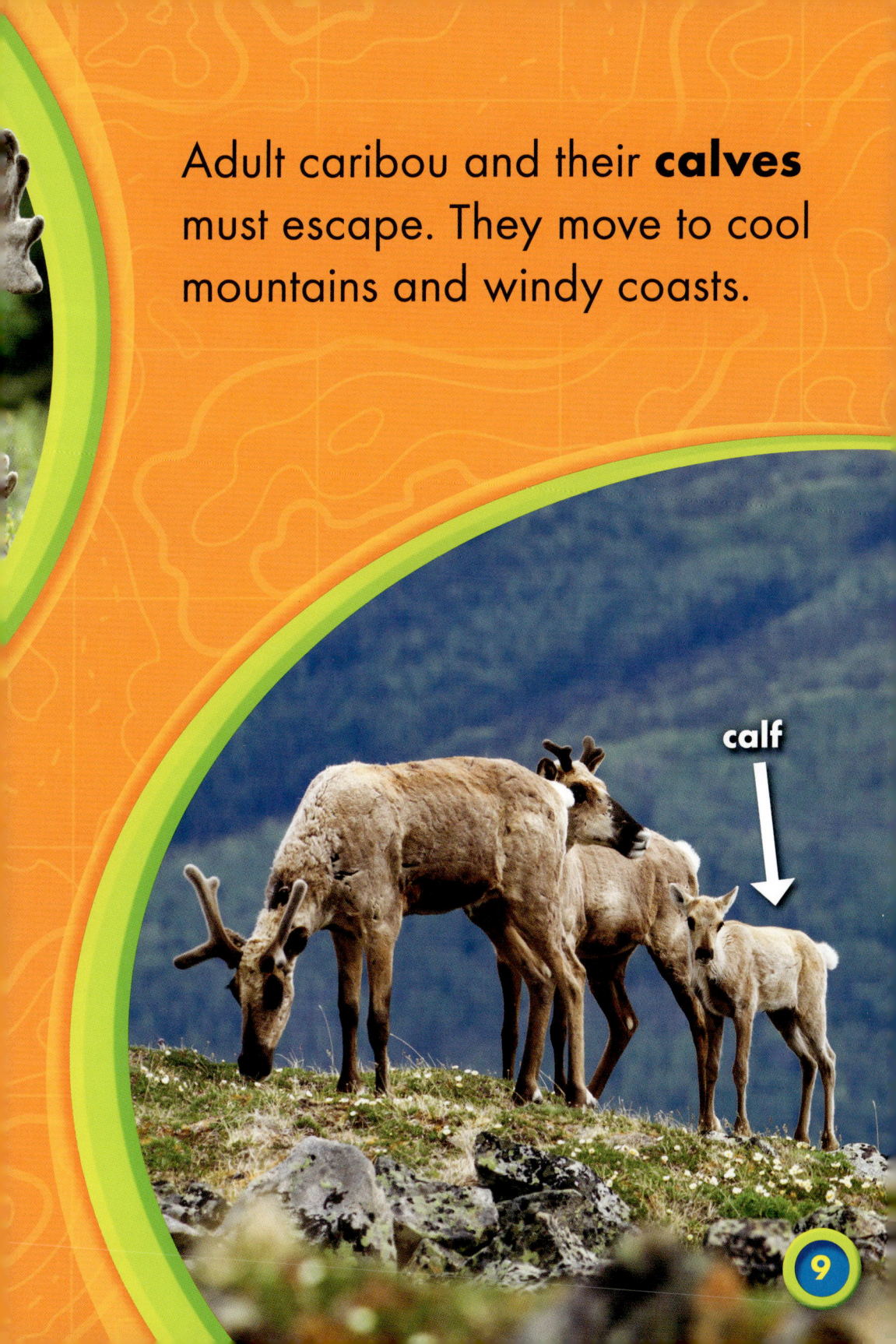

calf

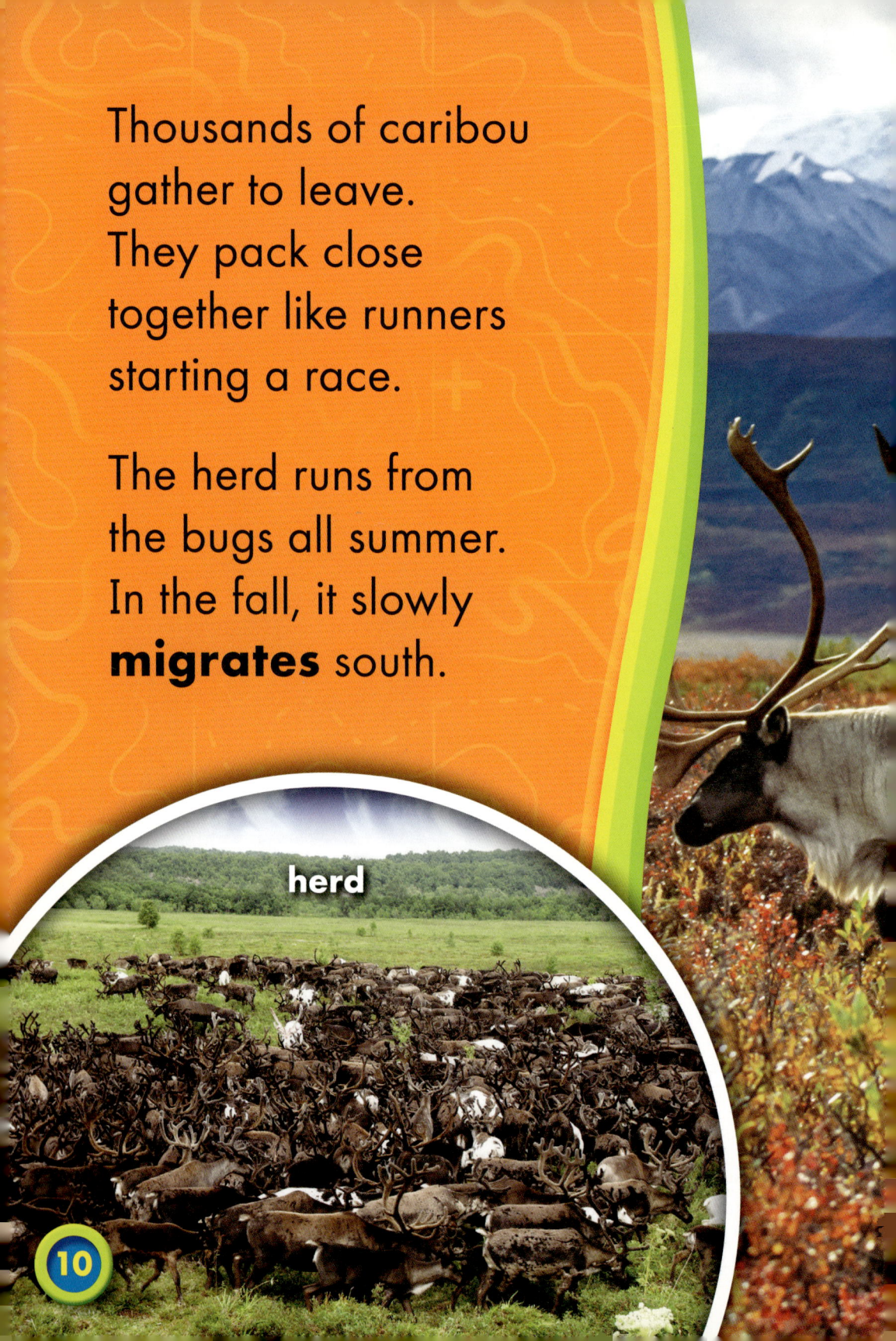

Thousands of caribou gather to leave. They pack close together like runners starting a race.

The herd runs from the bugs all summer. In the fall, it slowly **migrates** south.

herd

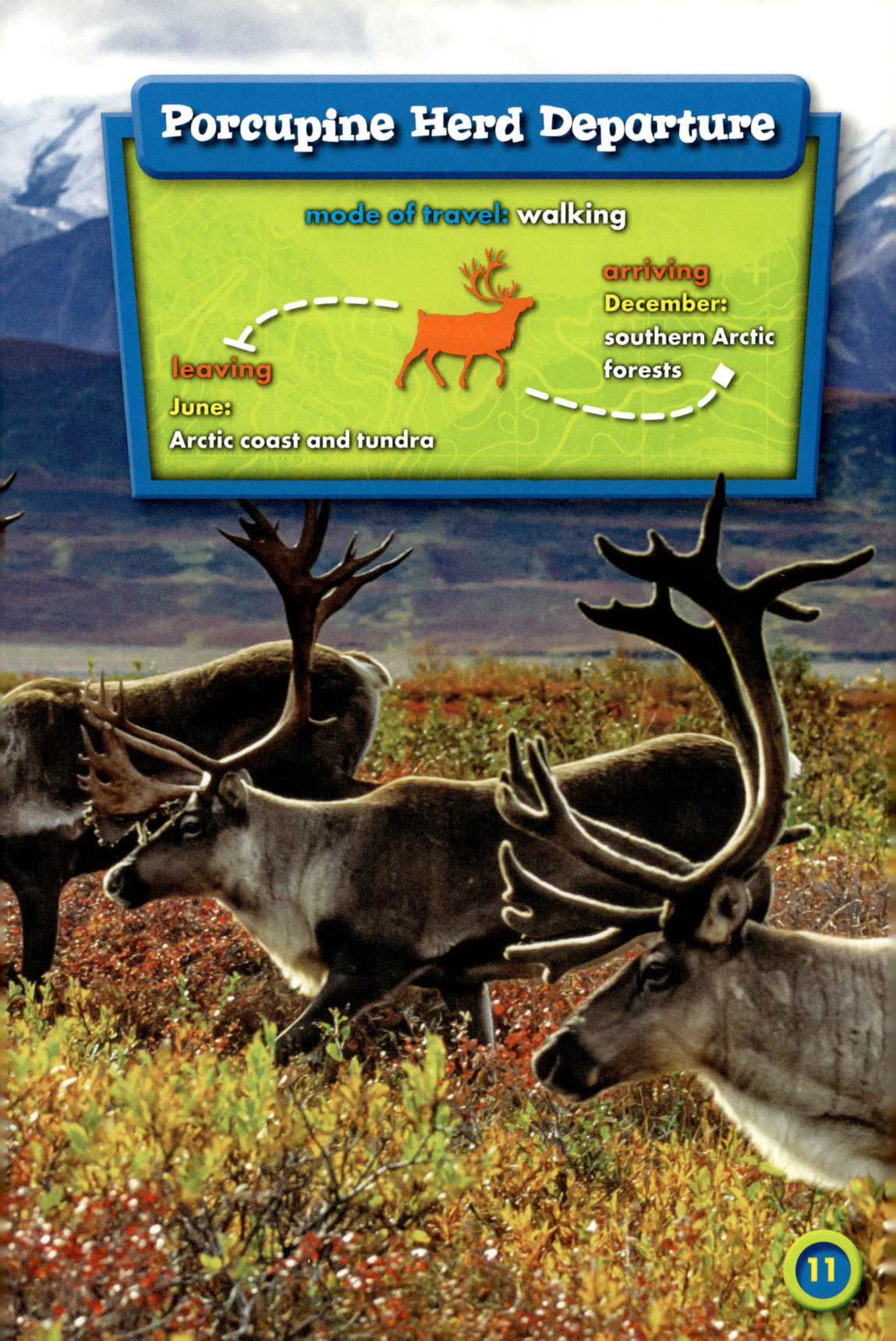

Porcupine Herd Departure

mode of travel: walking

leaving June: Arctic coast and tundra

arriving December: southern Arctic forests

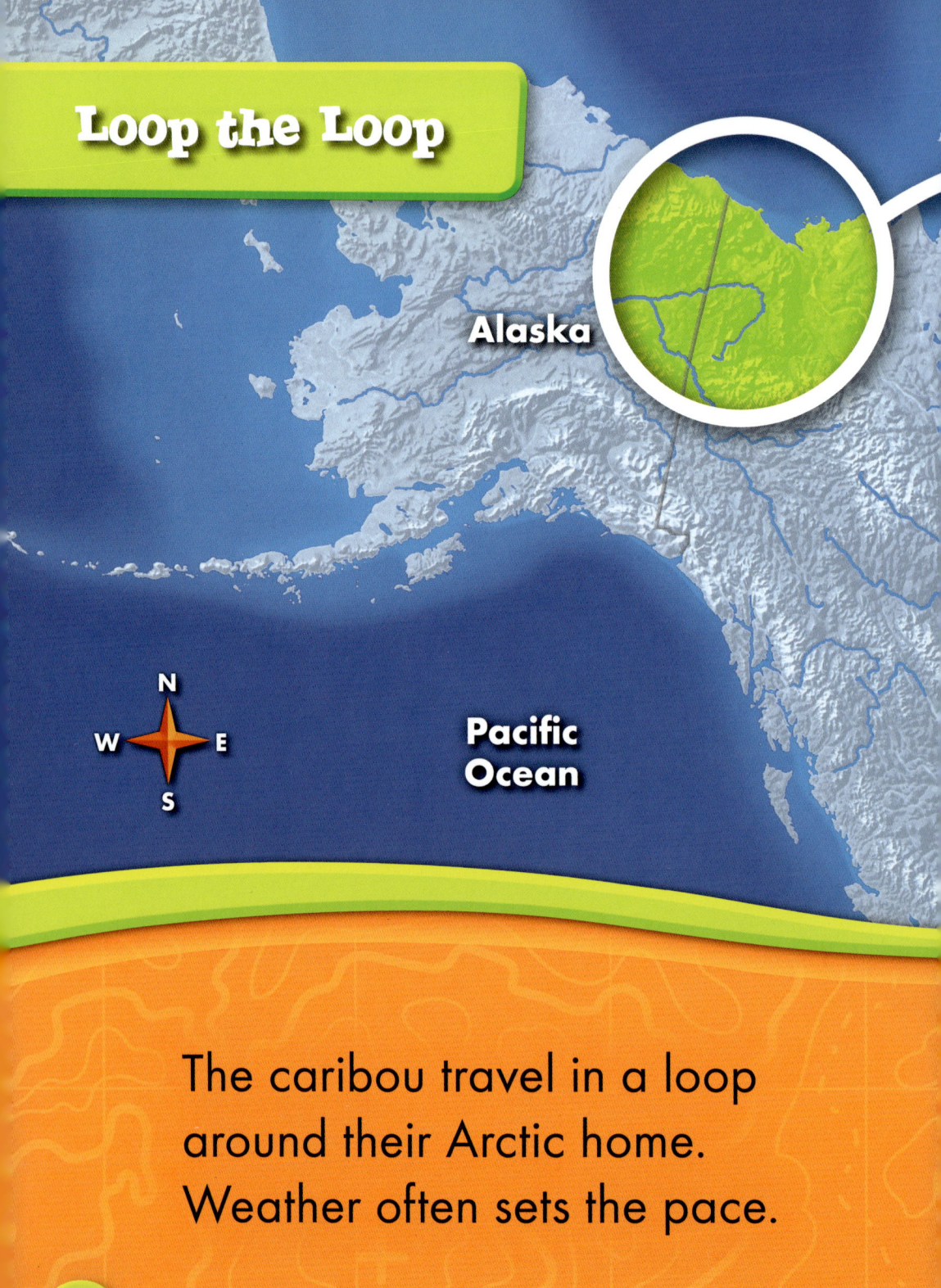

Loop the Loop

Alaska

Pacific Ocean

N W E S

The caribou travel in a loop around their Arctic home. Weather often sets the pace.

Porcupine Herd Migration

Legend:
- tundra
- forests
- departure trip (fall)
- return trip (spring)
- river

N W E S

0   50   100
miles

Canada

The herd moves faster when snow starts to fall. Its hungry members wind their way toward forests to find food.

antlers

In the fall, male caribou battle each other. They use their **antlers** to fight over females.

While they are busy, the herd becomes easier **prey** for wolves and bears.

By December, the caribou reach their winter home. They rest and eat **lichens** to gain weight.

lichen

Porcupine Herd Dashboard

speed: up to 50 mph (80 km/h)
mph = miles per hour   km/h = kilometers per hour

miles traveled per year:

-	3	0	0	0

(4,828 kilometers)

miles traveled per day:

-	-	-	1	6

(25 kilometers)

In April, **pregnant** females lead the way back to the tundra.

Summer Babies

The tundra's coast offers fresh food and cool breezes in early June. Female caribou use the area to give birth.

As they **nurse** their calves, moms look out for hungry **predators**.

nursing

Porcupine Herd Return

mode of travel: walking

leaving
April:
southern Arctic forests

arriving
June: Arctic coast
and tundra

Calves are able to run hours after birth. They can swim a few days later.

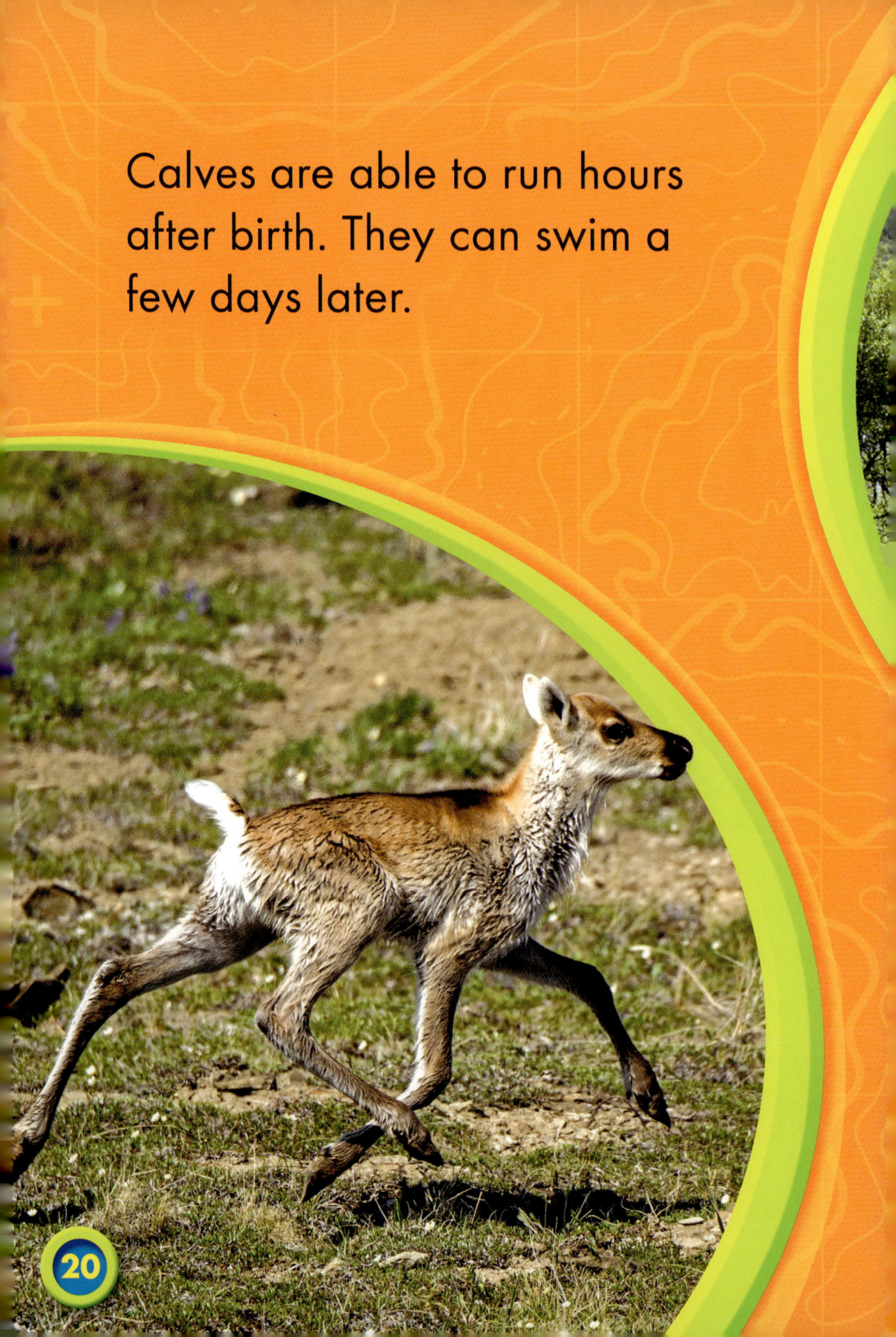

These skills will soon come in handy.
The calves will migrate with the herd
just weeks after being born!

Glossary

antlers—the branched horns on the head of a caribou

Arctic—the area around the North Pole

calves—baby caribou

herd—a group of caribou

hooves—hard foot coverings on the feet of caribou

lichens—plantlike growths that spread across ground, rocks, or trees

mammals—warm-blooded animals that have backbones and feed their young milk

migrates—travels from one place to another, often with the seasons

nurse—to give a baby milk to drink

predators—animals that hunt other animals for food

pregnant—expecting a baby

prey—animals that are eaten by other animals for food

spongy—soft and springy

tundra—a large, flat area in northern parts of the world where there are no trees and the ground is always frozen

To Learn More

AT THE LIBRARY

Borgert-Spaniol, Megan. *Caribou*. Minneapolis, Minn.: Bellwether Media, Inc., 2018.

Packham, Chris. *Amazing Animal Journeys*. New York, N.Y.: Sterling Children's Books, 2016.

Schuetz, Kari. *Life in a Tundra*. Minneapolis, Minn.: Bellwether Media, Inc., 2016.

ON THE WEB

Learning more about caribou migration is as easy as 1, 2, 3.

1. Go to www.factsurfer.com.

2. Enter "caribou migration" into the search box.

3. Click the "Surf" button and you will see a list of related web sites.

With factsurfer.com, finding more information is just a click away.

Index